Dr. Petra M. Beck

A Rescue Plan for President Obama

7 Steps to a Win-Win Economy

1. Reform the Lending System or Face a Revolt

2. Learn to Cope With Disruptive Change

3. Re-evaluate Orthodox Economic Theories

4. Apply Quality Management & Quality Awards to Measure Economic Performance

5. Make the Economic Rescue Plan Sustainable

6. Enhance Shareholder & Stakeholder Value Concepts with Government Support

7. Create Fair Free Trade

A Rescue Plan for President Obama

Author: Petra Beck

© Petra Beck 2008

ISBN 978-0-9811772-0-5

Published by Papyrus Publications Ltd., a member of IPAC
(Independent Publishers Association of Canada)
Suite #703,
105 – 150 Crowfoot Crescent NW,
Calgary Alberta Canada T3G 3T2

Printed and bound in Canada

Printed on 100% recycled paper

This book is dedicated to my grandparents

Acknowledgements

Numerous wonderful individuals helped me write and publish this book.

The tireless patience and hard work of my editor Rod Chapman made it possible to prepare the manuscript within an extremely tight timeframe of less than two months.

John Breeze introduced me to IPAC (Independent Publishers Association of Canada), printed the first review copies and designed the front cover.

Bryon and Ilona encouraged and inspired me.

My brilliant teachers at university and my superiors at work helped me interpret and make sense of the many challenges facing our world today.

Several publishers such as the biggest scientific publisher in Germany, Gabler, and the oldest publisher in the world and the management and marketing literature leader in Europe, Orell Fuessli in Zurich, Switzerland, have helped me to reach a wide audience of readers with the publication and promotion of my textbooks.

Of course, none of this could have been achieved without the support and understanding of my family, including my grandparents who both passed away years ago but who are still blessing me with their guidance every day.

Table of Contents

I. Introduction

The economic depression all over the world and the grim outlook for the future amounts to an enormous challenge to political leaders, central banks, banks, corporations and households. And if we don't act fast, the worst is yet to come: mass unemployment, poverty, escalating crime and violence, widespread pessimism and devastation.

This book proposes a way to get the economy back on track. The crisis at hand can only be solved at the local level. The solution requires several steps, starting with the introduction of lending units such as co-ops and credit unions working in parallel with the current banking system.

We have to learn from past mistakes. Deficit spending – or, to put it more simply, printing money – may help cure the symptom, but it does nothing for the disease. Investments in infrastructure can help sustain an economy, but the economy has to be healthy to begin with, otherwise the problems will resurface after the spending spree.

One of the main ideas in this book is to disregard the concept of costs in favor of the concept of activities that have value and are connected to entrepreneurial or individual goals. Property rights theory and the concept of activities are the theoretical building blocks of this analysis. Characteristics such as leadership, strategies, customer satisfaction, process management, empower-ment, resources information and analysis and financial results can be used to measure performance. These characteristics and their contribution in percentage points to an overall figure can already be found in American and European quality awards programs.

This book does not claim to offer a complete answer. There is an enormous lack of compatibility between applied accounting and reality. The change that has to occur has to tackle deep, underlying problems. But we should not let old, antiquated cost accounting and Shareholder Value systems ruin the lives of millions of people.

Unfortunately, we have now reached a point in the evolution of the current financial crisis where the crash of equity and home markets is turning into a form of expropriation – a terrible situation that will leave entire generations penniless and jobless.

We also have to look again at the past: mismanagement and overspending by public authorities can lead to inflationary pressures that worsen the crisis. A discussion about the validity of interest rates, the abuse of financial power and the need for regulation has been going on for thousands of years. Money was not imposed on us and money itself is not creating our problems – we are. Unfortunately, technology in the form of the Internet has increased the monetization of nearly everything, and at the same time it has increasingly depersonalized our interactions.

Yet I believe a change in our collective conscience is happening right now. It is telling us that we cannot continue like this. Every crisis can be looked at as a problem, or as a challenge for change. Let us look at this crisis as a historic learning experience, one that will lead the way to a better future.

This book shows the way. Although it cannot provide all the answers to all the questions being raised today, it can try to launch a much-needed discussion about the need for alternative methods to measure economic performance. Most important, it calls for a new economic theory.

We need a hands-on solution to help homeowners, corporations and individuals. The coordinated efforts have to be expanded to include the way banks are dealing with the escalating housing crisis affecting world capital markets and the world economy. If banks are not engaging to solve the crisis, grassroots non-profit organizations such as co-ops will have to be set up to diminish financial pressures at the local level. This bottom-up solution has to be supported by commitments from our leaders to start tackling the problems of Main Street – top down.

We have to learn from the past, in particular from the events during the Great Depression in the late 1920s and early 1930s when we saw double-digit unemployment rates, social unrest and starvation.

So far the coordinated interventions of central banks and governments as lenders of last resort have helped avoid a complete meltdown and collapse of markets internationally. Billions of dollars were pumped into the financial system worldwide. Banks are receiving incredible amounts of money to prevent market failure. Yet the goal of making them lend again has not been achieved. If billions of dollars are handed out to financial institutions, there have to be some strings and conditions attached to guarantee lending again.

We should stop putting ourselves and future generations at risk designing more and more rescue packages for institutions and creating more and more debt. We have to set up a regulatory panel to monitor the mortgage situation of individual homeowners – one that is ready to step in and restructure or change mortgage contracts already in place. Banks all around the globe were involved in the initial rescue attempts – the concept of a global banking solution in which banks modify or suspend existing mortgage contracts should be expanded and tied to a worldwide regulatory framework.

We all know that a home loan in Kentucky could have been secured with a German lender which in turn sold or insured that debt with an institution in Hong Kong. This interdependence led to the catastrophic accumulation of bank failures around the world. This domino effect can only be overcome with coordinated efforts from the banks. Governments and regulatory boards all over the world have to work together to slow down the fast and destructive pace of this crisis.

We can watch mortgages being renegotiated in some places. This can help, but it will come too late to stop the avalanche rolling toward us in the form of existing foreclosures – foreclosures that do not even show up yet on the balance sheets of banks.

We also have to consider setting up local and municipal institutions with governmental guidance and regulations – co-ops, credit unions and non-profit organizations – whose main and only goal is to provide liquidity at the grassroots level of the economy. As long as profit maximizing and risk minimizing is in play, no lending will occur in the present ailing environment.

To avoid social unrest, we have to learn to cope with disruptive change. The choice we have to make is between reform and revolt. Since the crisis has now spread from frozen credit markets, failing companies and foreclosing individuals to double-digit decreases in spending and investing, we have to plan a reform of the entire financial system. Stimulus packages and government spending cannot pull us out of the crisis – and if they do help, they come with a certain time lag.

Monetary reforms and restructuring of economies can lead the way. The German monetary reunification is a perfect example of change implemented at a rapid pace and prosperity brought back to a region through transfers not only of money, but also of know-how, labor and economic principles.

We have to look at old theories, and examine what their application to economic growth has done for us. We have to examine their value under the present circumstances.

Supply-side economics is based upon slashing costs, wages and interest rates in times of trouble until markets are balanced again. But specialization, unlike centuries ago, is not the name of the game anymore. It is generalization. Technology has changed the way we conduct business and the way we access information. Simultaneous engineering, for instance, makes it possible to connect all the stages of the production process to each other.

Demand-side economics is all about government spending. John Maynard Keynes, the economist who came up with the idea, also had in mind that governments should only spend in bad times by drawing on the monies they had saved in good times. Unfortunately, this did not happen – governments did not save when times were good. Canada is one of the few exceptions in the world.

If we continue to measure Shareholder Value as a derivative of profits, costs and discounted cash flow, we will witness many more corporate failures around the world. Shareholder Value is about quality management.

Corporate greed has been getting in the path of selling healthy products and providing good customer service. This greed has stirred the whole world into a downward spiral.

We must have a new economic theory of sustainability. We will have to decide whether we want to continue to please Wall Street at the expense of Main Street. Politicians around the world seem to be slowly realizing that fact now. The next step should be the implementation of a new economic model instead of dishing out more and more money.

Quality awards and their criteria – empowerment of employees (one of the best examples is WestJet, a Canadian airline known for its strong corporate culture), environmental impact strategies, process management leadership, business results and resources – could provide the foundation for a new evaluation of companies and their performance. With this tool, the failing concept of cost could also be re-evaluated and replaced when necessary.

The manipulation of accounting practices in which balance sheets are merely window dressing was (and is) a means of justifying enormous write-offs and of generating artificial profits for big corporations. At the same time, governments provided tax benefits to institutions that outsourced jobs at an incredible pace, literally wiping out entire industries. And these accounting tricks don't reflect the total reality – this transfer of wealth has been going on for decades.

A new theory has to consider not only Shareholder Value but also Stakeholder Value. Companies such as Sir Richard Branson's Virgin Airlines show that there can be a feedback loop and funding of environmental projects while doing business efficiently. The bottom line is that a business has to create a win-win situation for itself and for the members of society. Scandals such as the tainted milk scandal in China definitely do not increase profits in the long run, but they do destroy faith and confidence in that specific product as well as in the corporate leadership. The impact of company failures on resources in general and the population in particular – think Union Carbide – is an important factor that has been generously overlooked for too long, to all our peril.

Free trade has to be re-evaluated. Does child labor and prostitution constitute free trade? If we agree with that notion, we have not evolved past the early days of industrialization hundreds of years ago. Does free trade imply that millions of jobs are lost, costing economies billions of dollars but increasing corporate profits in the short run? Free trade has to be a win-win situation for everybody involved. At least, that's what theoretical economics told us for a long time.

Interestingly, economies such as China and India are facing the same financial challenges as the western world, because of the interdependent nature of our financial markets. Growth rates in markets such as China have already slowed considerably. Furthermore, all emerging markets are going to face rapidly deteriorating environmental issues, since they are growing at a pace that exceeds the development of western economies during the age of early industrialization. Western economies made their incredible explosion in growth possible by an unprecedented transfer of know-how. Therefore, it seems that we must consider a new approach to economic policy and theory for all of us.

II. The Situation

We are facing a global economic recession that threatens to spiral out of control. After credit markets froze, central banks and governments began decreasing interest rates and pumping billions of dollars into markets. Governments and treasury departments stepped in by bailing out failing banks and bankrupted companies. Finance ministers are still assuring investors that their funds are safe and that they will be guaranteed by governments in cases of market failure.

National and international meetings and efforts are focusing on taking over, nationalizing and subsidizing ruined banks and ailing companies such as Freddie Mac and Fannie Mae, AIG, Fortis, Hypo Real Estate and General Motors, Ford and Chrysler just to name a few. Central banks and governments are supplying the markets with enormous cash injections to stabilize the volatility and – worse – trying to save the whole system from collapse. Stock and bond markets are deleveraging, creating a vicious downward spiral. Just like in the Great Depression, banks seem unwilling to lend money and even small mergers are being turned down. At the same time, the actions of central banks as lenders of last resort are pushing down interbank lending rates and decreasing interest rates. Governments are continuing to take over institutions, thereby almost eliminating markets.

What could be the worst case scenario?

If China and other major US Bond holders are starting to sell their stakes in the US bond market, we could face a bond market collapse with the U.S. Federal Reserve as the only substantial buyer.

All government funding would come to a halt, leaving the world economy in the dark with a global banking system failure.

Then all the funding that was provided just would have bought us some more time, and that's all.

III. The Problem

At the end of the day, who will pay for all these guarantees?

When will the crisis end?

Governments and central banks have already spent trillions of dollars, but it does not seem to have prevented further global stock market deleveraging, or the loss of millions of jobs, or deflationary pressures for wages, interest rates, stocks, bonds and commodities markets. Even gold is declining because the US dollar has become a safe haven for funds in struggling economies in the Third World along with funds in industrialized nations.

We can definitely compare this crisis with the Great Depression in the 1930s when stock markets collapsed causing unprecedented disaster for millions of people around the globe. Disruptive patterns like this always occur when speculative bubbles bust. Centuries ago the price of tulips in The Netherlands exceeded thousands of dollars. In the Great Depression many stocks became worthless after being overvalued, leading to mass suicides of investors and widespread desperation for the general public.

The world and its stock markets cannot be a casino over an extended period of time. In the long run, markets always generate the truth about the real price.

Governments globally are trying to spend their way out of this disaster. Investment in infrastructure is hailed as the solution. But what will become of us – small businesses in particular – if banks continue to be unable to fuel the

11

economy making consumers and producers unable to spend?

I believe that there is a need for reform. We need a new economic theory to understand markets and to get the economy back on track.

It is clear that we cannot continue to increase debt, finance wars without end, carry structural imbalances such as health care and pension payments, and expropriate millions of people every day by displacing them in the Third World and ruining them financially in the industrialized world.

But what is the underlying problem to this situation? And what is the solution? Can money continue to be the only cure?

The crisis began with frozen credit markets and failing banks. Still today, everybody is blaming the banks and the housing market for the situation facing us.

But the collapse of the financial system and the erratic movements of stock and bond markets is only a symptom, not the disease. For almost two decades the banks fueled a bubble, a fake economy that had to bust sooner rather than later.

Housing values were constantly on the rise, creating a source of income through equity take-outs or through sales. During this process the loan-to-value ratio increased as banks created mortgages with negative amortization, increased the principal portions of loans, and lowered their standards and criteria to lend. In the world they created, growth could only be generated if home prices continued to increase.

When the bubble burst, an explosion of foreclosures and bankrupted homeowners led to a meltdown of banks and insurance companies that had to write off all that debt – debt that will never be paid back. The meltdown also affected insurers and other financial institutions that were backing up the risky positions on the balance sheets of the banks. After the United States government took over the two biggest mortgage lenders and partly nationalized the biggest insurer, AIG, everybody began to look to the government and its treasury for help. Meanwhile the crisis has affected the entire world, with no end in sight. Car sales are hitting rock bottom, jobs are disappearing and consumer spending is weakening.

Still, central banks continue to offer cheap money to banks. Governments around the world continue to assert their willingness to step in and take over. Governments are discussing stricter regulations and more disclosure for lenders, but will this end the crisis?

Economic disruptions like the Great Depression also led to more regulations, but the regulations they set down did not really affect the problems at hand and they came too late. The only significant improvement came after a new theory was proposed and implemented. That theory was deficit spending.

Meanwhile, the widespread belief that public authorities such as governments and banks can buy us out of this situation is slowly coming to an end. We are beginning to realize that corporate bailouts and efforts to pump more and more money into the economy with financial packages and government programs cannot alone be the cure. Monetary support is good, but it tends to cover up the real problem.

The real problem, one that we will face for a long time to come, is the outsourcing of hundreds of millions of jobs and the unwillingness to face real social issues such as upgrading education systems and dealing with competitive challenges by emerging economies.

For a long time the boom in the housing market covered up those issues. Home owners were borrowing against ever-increasing home values while speculators were renovating and flipping homes in a rising market. Banks in turn were financing those needs, selling the debt and refinancing themselves while increasing the underlying security. When home values began dropping, it was a true recipe for disaster. Since credit markets are internationally connected through the financing and refinancing of banks, a global meltdown was inevitable. The coordinated actions of governments and central banks around the world helped prevent an even worse breakdown, but will the world economy stop deteriorating if no further actions are taken?

IV. The Solution

1. Reform the lending system or face a revolt

Compared to the Great Depression when countries competed to devalue their currencies, the international coordination of efforts today has dramatically improved. Today we have:

- synchronized international rate cuts
- coordinated money-market intervention by central banks
- guaranteed interbank lending rates by govern-ments
- backup plans for foreclosures and failed insured mortgages

However, there has been no change to the discussion about how to cure the problem. Everybody is still trying to use demand- or supply-side mechanisms for change. In the 1920s, orthodox supply-side economic theories asked for a further reduction of prices, wages and interest until market forces gained equilibrium between supply and demand. But how low do wages have to go to reach "equilibrium" between supply and demand?

The supply-side perspective and its belief in market forces was questioned by worried unions and socialist parties, and this helped proponents of the demand side come to life in the 1930s. Demand-side economists began asking for government action and spending to boost the economy. However, most of the actions being taken to solve high unemployment levels and the resulting threat to wealth and growth were themselves of an inflationary nature, or they had no effect at all.

Some critics even insist that there were negative repercussions, such as a lethargic dependence on government action, or a crowding-out effect for the private sector.

Of course, the proposed solutions required government savings in better times to reduce deficits resulting from government spending in troubled times. But in fact, internationally a considerable reduction of debt never happened. Some rules and limitations to public debt were put in place, but generally these rules did not succeed due to the tempting nature of spending.

The lesson to be learned from the Great Depression is that the losses and the deleveraging we are witnessing today are comparable to what happened almost 80 years ago. From 1929 to 1932 the Dow Jones fell almost 90 percent, while today we have already seen contractions of 50 percent and more in some stock market values!

During the Great Depression devastation, hunger and violence were rampant. Since May 2008, the use of soup kitchens in the US has increased by 40 percent.

What this means is that we have to act fast! Real decisions have to be made to put the economy back on track. There is no time to lose. We cannot afford to wait until monetary policy becomes completely ineffective, with interest rates approaching zero putting an end to lending like in Japan in the 1990s. At an interest rate of zero, no bank will consider lending money because of the risk factors. At that point the banks would rather hoard money than work on their damaged balance sheets.

In a deflationary depression, banks can no longer serve their function of satisfying borrowers and lenders: borrowers who wish to expand the limits of their net worth, and lenders who wish to save their holdings without the risk of default.

Confidence has to be restored and credible political actions have to be taken. There are two alternatives: set up a non-profit credit union system, or reform the current monetary system.

Contrary to banks, credit unions always guarantee all deposits, because the members own the institution. The co-op idea in various forms has, in fact, successfully saved entire communities.

In 1988 the Carling-O'Keefe Brewing Company in Regina and Saskatoon, two cities in Canada, was experiencing serious problems. In 1989 Carling-O'Keefe announced a merger and said that the Saskatoon plant would be closed due to rationalization of operations.

That announcement triggered a struggle with the union. After unsuccessfully seeking another buyer and being denied financing by the banks, the employees bought the company when 15 people agreed to invest in the brewery after approaching the Saskatchewan Economic Development Association (SEDA) for financing. Reasonable financing in the form of a no-interest loan was provided by SEDA on the condition that the new entity would be formed as a regular business structure, not as a co-operative. The union had wanted to set up a co-operative, but they were forced to accept the government's terms.

Just one year after the closure was announced, Great Western Brewing Company Limited was incorporated. It had a regular business structure, and the union remained in place. Today, Great Western Brewing Company has become a thriving business, and a success story illustrating what can be accomplished when governments and companies are willing to co-operate. It is also an example of what can be done in a short timeframe.[1]

Chemainus, a small town in British Columbia, Canada, is a success story as well. About 25 years ago, when the entire village was in danger of being shut down, it became The Little Town That Did. In 1982, community members took advantage of a provincial grant to revitalize their downtown. The citizens whitewashed the sides of five downtown buildings and invited artists from all over the world to work on these big canvasses. The resulting murals were spectacular, and inspired even more downtown art. After many years of marketing their concept, now some 400,000 tourists a year come to admire 33 works of art covering the downtown buildings.[2] Today the town is faced with a new threat – the sawmill is closing – but nobody is worried.

Sometimes in history, when nothing else seems to work, reforms take place.

These reforms are usually clear breaks with the previous methods of doing things. When a reform occurs, it suggests that everything that happened in the past is over, and everything that is going to happen in the future will be part of a new system. A reform of this magnitude, however, has to be credible. In the current situation, it must be based on the application of new economic theory and policy.

The reunification of communist East Germany with capitalist West Germany can highlight part of the solution. The breakdown of East Germany started with demonstrations all over the country. President Honnecker had already given the army orders to shoot civilians when the political intervention of West Germany guaranteed a peaceful outcome. Revolt was turned into reform. But the cost was enormous.

At the time of harmonizing, the exchange rate between the eastern and western Deutsch mark increased from 1:10 to 1:1. This enormous injection of capital resulted in widespread criticism but ultimately led to a peaceful solution. Also, all available funds in banks and held by individuals were converted at the same rate. Billions were transferred for almost 20 years with at least 60 percent ending up in consumption and creating no real long-lasting effects on the economy.

With the latest infrastructure but a high unemployment rate, the former East Germany is now facing many problems that remain structural in nature. The migration of workers and entrepreneurs from west to east was able to temporarily buoy the economy, but in the long run reality always kicks in. Investors follow the best return for their money in terms of labor productivity, and labor productivity is still low in some regions of eastern Germany.

Are we willing to face a similar fate globally?

If our leaders continue to contribute zero attention to education and science, and if giant corporations continue to determine where to produce – the lower the cost the better, even if child labor is involved – there will be no end to this imbalance between production and consumption patterns in our world.

As well, spending money seems to be the price for avoiding turmoil and violence. Since labor productivity was low and real growth almost non-existent, governments seem to be trapped. They continue to spend billions of dollars around the world. Since the money is not really being earned but is still being consumed, we are creating a vicious circle. This "temporary" permanent fix gives the general public more purchasing power, but it does not really change the situation. Even more worrisome than this explosion of spending (and therefore enormous deficits) is the fact that we do not want to see what does not work in the long run anymore – deficit spending.

Keynes suggested more government spending to pull us out of the Great Depression. But he also said that in good times governments should save and build a surplus that would help eliminate financial problems in subsequent recessions. Obviously, very few governments around the world followed this simple formula.

Back then, governments were able to buy us out of economic disasters. But to get us out of the crisis today, we have to consider whether our entire banking system must be transformed.

One characteristic of co-operatives and credit unions is that these institutions focus on the well-being of members within their communities. This close contact at the local level gives them important information about the needs and goals of their members – information that they can pass up to the provincial and federal levels. In turn, members borrowing from a local lender will want to pay back their debt and stay on good terms with the credit union.

A competition between these credit unions and their facilities can provide considerable positive change. Municipal guarantees can support this process.

More stable co-ops will attract more investors and lenders so that more money can be lent, and the economy can again expand.

This bottom-up approach has to be complemented by top-down monitoring. Regulation of these competing and parallel lending systems is essential to avoid any misuse, and because of the inflationary threat they might exercise.

The introduction of the Euro made the European Union a stronger trading unit in terms of an increased currency volume. At the same time, competitiveness increased between regions within Europe, and between their counterparts worldwide.

The same model could be implemented throughout other parts of the world, creating opportunities for growth. But the breakdown of economies worldwide shows how far away we are from being able to implement more currency zones similar to the Euro zone. In reality, the US dollar has become the world currency because of its promise of political stability. In Europe, the Deutsch Mark used to be (and is still in circulation in some Eastern European countries), and the Swiss Franc still is, considered to be the most stable currencies. Ideally, we should simply let the strongest and best currency take over the world currency exchange.

2. Learn how to cope with disruptive structural change

What caused this economic crisis to happen? Disruptive structural change occurs when production patterns and property rights change to an extensive degree. The transition from an agricultural society to an industrial society in the earlier part of the last century is one example. Another example may be seen today in the transition from industrialization to technology. This transition, however, seems to imply the emergence of speculative bubbles that render the banking system powerless.

Starting in the early 1990s until the widening of the crisis in 2007, banks were financing a housing bubble and therefore they subsidized many related industries as well. A lot of people were making a lot of money – until market forces kicked in. It is obvious that a big part of the general public was focused on buying and selling homes, renovating and flipping them, and taking equity out for personal consumption.

What happened to the rest of the economy?

First, an enormous number of jobs were outsourced and transferred overseas, where labor was cheaper. This transfer created unprecedented growth in markets such as China and India while at the same time our economies were still booming... huh? In other words, we had a fake economy producing only very temporary growth. We got lost in greed nurtured by the illusion of ever-rising stock and housing markets. Shareholder value was the theme of the day. Lowering costs and increasing demand were songs the corporate world was chanting.

23

When I witnessed the transfer and investment of billions of dollars in India and China and saw their stock markets celebrating these events, I could not help but wonder about the consequences to the workers at home in North America. But who cared, since the stock markets were still going up and up and up? The banking system simply responded by fueling the economy – but which economy?

The "left over" economy. The housing market.

Early warning signs such as the collapse of ENRON, Worldcom and others were widely ignored, with many observers blaming the greed of CEOs and, later, inappropriately regulated banks. Antiquated accounting systems enabled this state of blind ignorance and false security to continue for a while. After all, the banks believed in values that did not exist while investors and companies took advantage of huge cost write-offs and artificial profits that were widely accepted by the banks.

Let's put the problem in more analytical terms. The composition of costs and therefore profits has changed over the past century. Transaction- and information-related costs have increased compared to production costs. This shift has consequences for the evaluation of companies and their performance. The firm and its business transactions are based on activities that are allocated and distributed via the assignment of property rights. A new economic theory and evaluation of the economy in general and the firm in particular has to take these elementary considerations into account.

Facing this shift in the composition of costs and uncertainty such as we have in the current global situation, banks are not willing to take on more risk. Even though

24

banks are receiving low-interest, guaranteed, government-backed interbank refinancing, and billions are being spent around the world to bail them out and to supply them with the means to lend again, banks are reluctant and unwilling to fuel the economy like they did before the crisis hit.

This situation has occurred before, during the Great Depression.

The corporate credo of maximizing profits and minimizing risk is driving the banking system into its current state of passiveness. It does not make any sense to give more and more money to the banks if there is no more lending. You can lead a horse to water, but you cannot force it to drink. The absence of lending can lead to a breakdown of production.

This enormous disruption can be only cured with another disruption. To re-establish lending, new institutions have to be formed under the guidance of a regulatory board established with a mandate to ease lending. These institutions could take the form of co-ops, credit unions with local memberships and only local exposure, or non-profit organizations. Competition at a local level from non-profit lenders would lead to more competition, and therefore more lending, without pumping more money into the economy and threatening a devaluation of our currencies.

Furthermore, all theories that have been applied in economic policy in the last century have to be checked for effectiveness.

3. Reevaluate Orthodox Economic Theories

Supply-Side Theory

For centuries, Adam Smith's inquiry into the wealth of nations has been considered one of the foundations of economics.[3] According to his theory, the key to growth is specialization, or the division of labor.

"...the trade of a pin-maker: a workman not educated to this business... nor acquainted with the use of machinery employed in it (to the invention of which the division of labor has probably given occasion), could scarce, perhaps, with his utmost industry, make one pin a day, and certainly could not make 20. But in the way in which this business is now carried on, not only the whole work is a peculiar trade, but it is divided into a number of branches, of which the greater part are likewise peculiar trades. One man draws out the wire, another straightens it, a third cuts it, a fourth points it, a fifth grinds it at the top for receiving the head; To make the head requires two or three distinct operations; to put it on is a peculiar business, to whiten the pins is another; it is even a trade by itself to put them into the paper..." [4]

Today, most of this "peculiar work" is done by machines. The organization of labor and its generalization are the consequences of the information age and the dominance of technology.

Process management has changed dramatically. Simultaneous engineering guarantees better outcomes because of the interaction of research, production and marketing during production. A product can be improved

27

and evaluated for its market response before it is even marketed.

The concept of opportunity costs is crucial to an understanding of Smith's approach. Opportunity costs compare the next possible alternative when choosing one specific action over another. The defining moment of costs is supposed to be the least expensive alternative in any given setting. For example, if a secretary can type letters faster than a professor, then the opportunity costs of him not teaching are higher than the opportunity costs of the secretary. That's why costs became the decisive factor for specialization.

Unfortunately, our concept of costs and accounting is still based on these findings. They are still accurate, but they should be only applied to economies and to companies that use mass production. Today's focus is on generalization among information workers (everybody should know as much as possible about the product). Technology such as the Internet is facilitating these changes. Branding of products and services, emotional marketing, reputation and quality management have diversified markets that offer a huge variety of products. There are thousands of car models to choose from now, instead of Henry Ford's one and only Tin Lizzy.

Mass production is not the only means and driver of economic growth any more.

Diversity is the key to success in many markets. A proper evaluation of product diversification in the automobile industry would take into account a very different environment (higher fuel costs and pollution) and would include quality standards and not just cost advantages.

In the world of Adam Smith, money was primarily a means of exchange, of transaction and storage of value. Both of these characteristics still apply to the use of money. But money has also become a means of speculation and it is being stored and moved with electronic banking transactions. Computers even make it easier – almost effortless – to acquire, dispose and sell services and products.

"The real price of everything, what everything really costs to the man who wants to acquire it, is the toil and trouble of acquiring it. What everything is really worth to the man who has acquired it, and who wants to dispose of it or exchange it for something else, is the toil and trouble which it can save to himself, and which it can impose on other people. What is bought with money or with goods is purchased by labor, as much as what we acquire by the toil of our own body. That money or those goods indeed save us this toil." [5]

Labor itself has changed over the centuries. Technology has replaced the need to have all production stages and facilities near each other. Information is free, and communication comes at a much cheaper price.

According to Smith, labor was the first price, the original purchase-money, that paid for all things. "It was not by gold or by silver, but by labor, that all the wealth of the world was originally purchased; and its value, to those who possess it and who want to exchange it for some new productions, is precisely equal to the quantity of labor which it can enable them to purchase and demand."[6]

Smith concludes that labor is difficult to measure and evaluate, so that money has become the instrument to estimate value.[7] [8]

A different reality demands different rules of the game! Therefore, the way we measure and evaluate economic performance has to be changed. It is narrow-minded to look at profits and discounted cash flows when in fact quality determines the outcome of production, management and research.

With the increasing use of money, the issue of the stability of the demand for money has also become an important factor for the growth of an economy. In the classical approach to the economy, central banks are able to control monetary supply by manipulating interest rates. If, however, monetary demand is changed – or worse, being disrupted like it is today – central banking and the banking system as a whole become increasingly unable to produce effective remedies for ailing economies. The problem is that the quantity of goods and services being exchanged has to be served by an appropriate amount of money. With more and more money in circulation for the same amount of goods and services being exchanged, the real and nominal prices tend to diverge. This is the ultimate threat to a healthy economy. Money becomes worthless.

Technology paved the way from a specialized world with a division of labor to a generalized world with synergies of labor. As a consequence, the use of money also changed. Accounting practices and evaluation, however, have not changed.

So what justifies looking at Shareholder Value in the same way we looked at it a century ago?

Science has just started to look at the qualitative effects of a changing environment with New Institutional Economics, whereas quantitative measures are still mainly assigned to government and central bank actions. This gap between perception and reality has led to profound misunderstandings of the economic environment we are living in.

A proper answer to the problem of economic downturns – and specifically depressions – has to focus on an attempt to evaluate business performance, or simply the changed world of labor. Furthermore, the analysis of economic performance must discern between qualitative and quantitative effects or, in Adam Smith's words, nominal and real prices.

First, for the sake of obtaining a complete picture, we have to discuss the phenomenon of disturbances to economic growth analyzed using existing theoretical contributions in economics. In economics, two perspectives are generally considered – the supply side and the demand side.

In recent decades a paradigm shift occurred as we began to focus more on informational issues when evaluating economic situations. This recent paradigm shift was based on criticism of the behavioral assumptions of orthodox economic theories, mainly the assumption of perfect information access by all participants. As J.E. Stiglitz, a Nobel-prize-winning economist, wrote in 2002 in the *American Economic Review*, "Information can have adverse effects on volatility. And information can lead to the destruction of markets, in ways which lead to adverse effects on welfare."[9]

But there is also the impact of trust, of a change of values (in other words, property rights) to be considered. Much more work is to be done, and it better be done fast.

Orthodox Neoclassical Economics claims that prices and costs are the main factors that decisions makers must take into account when taking economic action. According to Stiglitz, "The argument of Adam Smith (1776) that free markets lead to efficient outcomes 'as if by an invisible hand'…suggested that we could, by and large, rely on markets without government intervention….The paradigm seemed to say that unemployment did not exist, and that issues of efficiency and equity could be neatly separated… institutional arrangements left unexplained. The implication was that unemployment would be eliminated if markets were more flexible, that is, if unions and government interventions were eliminated. Even if wages fell by a third in the Great Depression, they should have, in this view, fallen even more."[10]

But, in fact, almost all prices and wages are fixed and regulated by contracts, specific laws and other kinds of agreements.

In the beginning of the last century, supply-side economics implied the assumptions of neoclassical theory – perfect foresight and perfect information of all market participants, and rational behavior. This idealized perspective of a world without transaction costs or friction led to demands and hotly criticized political actions. The neoclassical approach and its agenda in the 1930s is best described by looking at the economic analysis at that time. The following comments are by a well-known economist, John Emmett Kirshman:

"After complete failure to cartellize industry and thus control production, the government sought to remedy the disequilibrium in the price structure through the easing of money and credit and the improvement in government finances. Credit is claimed for the adjustment of the supply of commodities to the demand, for restoration of the equilibrium between agricultural and industrial prices, and for the balancing of the value of exports against imports. However, complete failure is admitted in the attempt to adjust prices and costs owing to the rigidity of wages and interest." [11]

Demand-Side Theory – Deficit Spending

John Maynard Keynes challenged this view by addressing the rigidity problem with government action. The government could organize the markets in a way that would sustain consumption, investment, employment and growth. Keynes questioned the discussion of the trade cycle and proposed a new approach to the problem of unemployment and inflation.

The price we had to pay for governments not reducing debt during good times is clear. Keynes's idealistic application of the theory would have reduced debt levels in economically good times. That was his idea of anti-cyclical policy. *The General Theory of Employment, Interest and Money* written by Keynes in 1936 was one of the most revolutionary books ever published.[12] His book represents a turning point between the old neoclassical school and the economics practiced thereafter. The neoclassical perspective that market forces would take care of every disturbance, such as a decline in wages, was severely challenged by Keynes:

"The volume of employment is uniquely correlated with the volume of effective demand measured in wage units, and that the effective demand, being the sum of the expected consumption and the expected investment, cannot change, if the propensity to consume, the schedule of marginal efficiency of capital and the rate of interest are all unchanged. If without any change in these factors, the entrepreneurs were to increase employment as a whole, their proceeds will necessarily fall short of their supply price... the individual entrepreneur, seeing his own costs reduced, will overlook at the outset the repercussions on the demand for his product and will act on the assumption that he is able to sell at a profit a larger output than before. If, then, entrepreneurs generally act on this expectation, will they in fact succeed in increasing their profits? Only if the community's marginal propensity to consume is equal to unity, so that there is no gap between the increment of income and the increment of consumption."[13]

Although Keynes admits that a reduction of wages will decrease prices somewhat, he says it will also lead to a redistribution of income and concludes that this will have a negative impact on the propensity to consume.[14] In the case of an open economy, he argues, a reduction of wages will worsen the terms of trade since the change will be favorable to investment. In the end, there will be a reduction in real incomes.[15]

Growing demand from consumers leads, all other factors being equal, to an increase in corporate profits. But how can we determine the value of a company that is facing decreasing demand from its customers? Economic contraction and decreasing economic activity has always been something to fear. This psychological component tends to aggravate the situation. A closer look at consumer behavior and history shows that we facing the same problems today, only at another level and with other characteristics.

The Great Depression in the 1930s was caused by speculation financed with credit, lender liquidation and mismanagement. During the depression the number of stockholders was increasing, and banks were flooding the economy with money. But the less stable an economy, the more risk will be contained in speculative activity.

Starting in the United States in 2007, speculation in the housing market has taken the banking system to its knees. The previous 10 or more years of economic disruption and outsourcing of jobs was a major reason why so many people engaged in real estate speculation. Many scholars are convinced that speculation can be seen as a cause of the cycle, a result, a characteristic and a process of getting into a depression, as well as a way of getting out.[16]

Lack of liquidity in the stock markets led to a downward trend, with stocks constantly bouncing up and down. Money markets have been doing better because of the coordinated actions taken by the world's leading economies:

Coordinated central bank interest rate cuts

Promises that bank deposits are safe

Efforts to create, stabilize and guarantee interbank lending markets

Being aware of the interdependence of global financial markets is already a great improvement compared to the ineffective measures that were taken during the Great Depression, such as currency devaluation. After bubbles burst, market forces are unclear, unfocused and disrupted. If traders and investors are discouraged, markets can easily go into a downward spiral because everybody wants to sell. With no more credit, markets can turn into free fall.

Indeed, several stock exchanges (Moscow and Hong Kong, for example) just stopped trading to prevent the worst. But suspension of trading is not a suitable tool to encourage markets. In downward swings, intervening technical supportive derivatives, anxious to conserve rapidly shrinking assets, force the market even lower.[17]

This issue includes hedge funds that were designed to reduce risks by buying or selling the opposite position in the market. But what if there is no more opposite position, and the market turns into a one-way street heading south? After becoming aware of these risks, a hearing in the United States in November 2008 concluded that the use of these derivatives has to be restricted for the sake of a more stable market.

Change in the distribution of income is normally accompanied by a change in the character of markets. This is, without a doubt, creating a discord between different groups of society, such as shareholders and CEOs, companies and banks, employers and employees. This change in the property rights structure implies a serious economic disturbance.

Getting back to consumers, less spending leads to less profit for companies, and less profit leads to cuts in the workforce. Today, lower wages are leading to more part-time jobs and decreasing incomes.

Bertrand Nogaro, a leading French economist, identified the decreased purchasing power of the agricultural classes as an important cause of the depression in the 1930s.[18] With the publication of the general theory of Keynes, deficit spending by governments seemed to be a way out. One of the worst implications of a deflationary scenario is what Keynes described as the liquidity trap. A general lack of trust will cause people to hold cash rather than interest-bearing bonds that might later lose their value. Then, monetary policy and changes in interest rates would not have any impact on unemployment. Increased consumption via increased government spending, he suggested, would lead to more trust and prosperity. Of course, people have to believe that this is truly a solution.[19]

But in fact, it worked. Ever since then, governments have been spending money to help the economy. Additionally, there are some crowding-out effects to consider.

Increasing government debt leads to fears of increasing taxes, according to Milton Friedman. Brunner and Meltzer also consider the public sector to be less efficient than the private sector. Nevertheless, the Keynesian approach seemed to work until it was challenged by increasing oil prices in the early 1970s.

In the 1970s the Phillips curve (which postulates that the lower the unemployment rate in an economy the higher the rate of increase in wages) suggested that an expansive monetary policy, even with the acceptance of inflation, would lead to a higher employment rate. But this relationship turned out to be inconsistent over time, and – of course – governments were not able to buy their way out of unemployment.

In general, Keynes and Keynesians do not attribute much power to monetary policy, which is still being disputed by monetarists today. One of the crucial assumptions for an effective monetary policy is the stability of the demand for money. Usually, Keynesians look at the relation between short-term interest rates and the demand for money, and come to the conclusion that the demand for money is unstable. Consequently, for them, monetary policy measures are not effective.

Monetarists, however, tend to rely more on the long-term relationship between interest rates and the demand for money. Their conclusion is of course that monetary policy is effective.

With interest rates being cut around the world at an enormous pace, central banks are becoming more and more powerless. At rates at or near the zero mark, there will be no more lending. At the same time, with bond market yields going down, there will be no more demand for government bonds, and government spending will come to a halt all over the world.

Of course, psychological factors in the marketplace are further deteriorating the picture. In his book, *The Fed: The Inside Story of How the World's Most Powerful Financial Institution Drives the Markets,* Martin Meyer gives a comprehensive overview of how a central bank works in reality.[20]

Disruptive change like that can only be met and cured with disruptive change.

A clear distinction has to be made between the financial and monetary systems that we have had up to this point, and the systems that we need to put in place for the future.

I believe that community-based co-operative credit facilities in a new denomination will be willingly accepted. Programs developed on a local basis will be more self-reliant, and they will support each other with business activities. As in the aftermath of all monetary reforms, every person should receive a startup amount of money. It is along these lines that credibility can again be restored.

A new economic theory has to acknowledge that institutions do matter, and that information is not available for everybody at the same time, as Keynesian and neoclassical approaches suggest. The basics of this new theoretical approach to the economy has to incorporate the importance of changing property rights – people become members of banks, and companies have a greater incentive to perform.

New Institutional Economics

Douglass C. North, who shared the Nobel prize in economics in 1993, showed that activities and property rights can explain the different performance of companies in communism and capitalism. In communism, certain activities are assembled and conducted within a specific timeframe to meet a predetermined "plan," whereas in capitalism the goal seems to be profit maximization. Both ideologies are based on a theory emphasizing activities as the foundation of economic conduct, not profit or costs.

New Institutional Economics and its contributions apply property rights and activities to economic analysis.[21] The main thesis is that institutions do matter, and that the costs they absorb imply specific economic results. Organizational structures and their specific set of property rights can be designed in a way that guarantees the least-costly allocation and distribution of resources. So, depression can be looked at as an externality that has to be internalized by the "appropriate" allocation and distribution of property rights.

Basically, this theory suggests that every economic problem is caused by a bias between property rights assignments and the choices they imply. In practical terms, that means giving away millions of jobs and know-how to be replaced by cheaper imported goods. This, in turn, means declining growth rates in the long run, as well as radical change in the allocation and distribution of property rights.

Unfortunately, corporate decisions are not based on these realities but simply on the maximization of profits for that particular corporation. Since New Institutional Economics is a relatively new field, its core definitions and ramifications are still being discussed. However, according to Stiglitz a paradigm shift has just taken place considering the appropriate evaluation of information in economics.

But New Institutional Economics is not focused on information alone. It also discusses the importance of behavioral patterns, incentives, evolutionary aspects and transaction costs. So far, very few contributions have indicated the real value of economic choices in terms of economic success and failure as expressed in comparable figures. It has been determined, though, that the institutional setting and its changes determine the efficiency of an organization. Unfortunately, the term *efficiency* is vague, and its definition depends heavily on the economic setting being considered.

Fact is that transformation from the age of industrialization to the information age requires a new approach to the measurement of economic performance. In other words, if the content of the property rights an institution is based on is changing, its value is changing as well. As a consequence, the rules of the game have to be changed to allow significant improvement of economic performance.

Selling a car involves a great deal of effort in marketing today, compared to 100 years ago when only a single model was produced and selling it did not require much advertising. From an accounting perspective, a car is part of the equipment of a firm – it is represented by its original cost and its depreciation over time. However, this approach does not give us any information regarding the use of the car. Is the car being used to create a write-off to reduce corporate profits, or is it contributing to generate income?

The concept of cost makes it hard to evaluate different settings, since it is already based on a two-way definition: opportunity cost – the cost of the next best alternative. In contrast, activities tell us about the real action being taken in any given situation. Only when we understand this are we able to conduct a proper evaluation of economic performance.

If shareholders are granted transferable rights in a share, but have no say if it comes to the distribution of the capital owned by the firm, there will be no incentive for them to buy more shares. After the collapse of Nortel in Canada the CEO, John Roth, received a golden parachute of $70 million – and shareholders were left with the dwindling market value of their shares.

Who will buy shares if there are no more dividends? The relationship between the allocation, distribution and assignment of property rights is another key to understanding why problems such as deflation can appear.

We have entered the information age without a concept of measuring the brand capital of a company – its network and reputation. When lending money, banks still look only at what a company owns in terms of property – cars, equipment, buildings, capital savings and outstanding debt. This is certainly understandable because lenders want to be sure they can seize assets in case of bankruptcy. But what about the potential of that company?

Recent stock market performance has shown that cash flow alone is not a valid indicator for the overall evaluation of a company. Do we really know enough about the Key

Success Factors (KSFs) of a company, or even of an economy?

Had costs been evaluated properly, maybe the current crisis could have been resolved in a different manner.

In the 1920 and 30s corporations accumulated large stocks of material for years with the aid of credit and government valorization. Of course, these inventories produced immense write-offs for the companies, leaving them with low profits and low taxes. This, in turn, created an incentive not to hire more employees, thus driving wages down with all the negative repercussions on consumption. On the other hand, the financial support of the banking system (unregulated at that time by the government) led to an incredible bubble that grew bigger and bigger, since investors still believed in fast profits at the stock markets.[22]

Mismanagement of large corporations caused the situation to deteriorate as well. Based on information provided by receivers, experts, committees or special investigating groups, empirical studies about the causes of the crisis in the 1930s conclude that ineffective management caused the bond default.[23] Doesn't this remind you of the junk bond era, and other recent events?

Surprisingly, the rural population was not really affected by the crisis.[24] The transformation from an agricultural to an industrial economy might help to explain that fact. But what about the situation today?

Today, we are facing the consequences of a shift from an industrial to an information-oriented society. The fact that costs are highly interdependent is becoming more and more threatening, because of the more pronounced value of information in this new era. In other words, we have become aware that costs do not reflect reality.

John Joseph Wallis and Douglass C. North argue that from 1870 to 1970 transaction costs became perhaps more important than production costs. The GNP transaction-cost percentage more than doubled, rising from 26.09 to 54.71 percent, mainly because of the increasing cost of specifying and enforcing contracts, the effect of technological change in production and transportation, and the declining cost of using the political system to restructure property rights. [25]

Walter Y. Oi confirms that of the total man-hours worked to produce goods in 1900, only 11 percent was used in the US distribution process. By 1980, however, that figure had climbed to 61 percent.[26]

In the information age, the focus has shifted from production and specialization to transportation, distribution, financing and generalization to generate more demand and profits. Institutions and their organizational arrangements have become more important to conducting business. Business leaders are confronted with the challenge of variety instead of volume. Everything seems to have changed, except our notion of the concept of costs. More than ever, we need to look at business activities.

If we look at costs derived from the old accounting rules, the concept of Shareholder Value (SV) has to be questioned and perhaps even modified. If costs go up, the profits a company makes and the discounted cash flow it generates will vanish, along with its SV. On the other hand, increasing transaction costs can lead to an increase in profitability. SV based on a simple equation such as profits is valid as a concept only as long as increasing profits implies a less-expensive labor force and less expensive input with the same output.

Stephen F. O'Byrne even says that a negative cash flow can be an indicator of a rapidly growing business. He suggests converting free cash flow into a meaningful measure of periodic performance, but he continues to focus on discounted cash flow as the main notion of an investment decision.[27]

Traditional accounting does not reflect the element of risk, or the allocation and distribution of property rights, and it is based on a cost concept that was set up 150 years ago. A look at history shows that the separation of production and transaction costs seemed to be right in the age of industrialization, since the organization of key input factors was fairly simple. Adam Smith is considered to be the father of economics. In his classic book, *An Inquiry into the Nature and Causes of the Wealth of Nations,* which changed our understanding of the economic world, Smith showed that specialization was a key input factor.

Now, however, it is a few hundred years later and we have entered another era. Assembly lines and repetitive jobs are being replaced by computers and robots. Computerization makes many jobs – even some in transportation and communication – obsolete. In the information age, most jobs that can be automated are being eliminated from the job market.

In the age of industrialization, with the dominance of production costs and the principle of substitution between units of labor and capital, not much choice was involved in organizing an institutional arrangement. Now, the idea that transaction and production costs are highly independent, and consequently hard to measure, has called into question our existing accounting systems. Transaction costs play a dominant role in economic decisions, since labor productivity has increased and seems to be dependent on specific organizations.

Generalization is a key approach today. Customers can conduct many transactions by themselves on the Internet, including booking tickets, making reservations, buying groceries, banking and trading in the stock market.28 Concepts such as depreciation, appreciation and costs in general need to be redefined. Antiquated taxation systems have lead to incredible losses at the government level, with negative repercussions for the economy. Cosby's concept of cost of deviation and coherence from a specific goal seems to be a far better approach to deal with an evaluation of economic activities.

Generalization is important for the information worker, since specialized knowledge can be acquired at very little cost. But the disadvantage is that in terms of costs we are looking at a different scenario. Again, all costs are highly interdependent. The cost of organization influences the amount of production costs. In communism, organizational costs were so prohibitively high that production levels just kept things on an even keel. On top of that, there was no incentive to produce more.

In franchising, high organizational costs guarantee a specific product or service. No matter where the client is, he or she is assured of standardized quality. Unfortunately, while increased costs can lead to more customer appreciation, the amount of cost does not really tell us whether a business decision is effective.

In times of specialization, when each worker had only one specific task to do, an increase in organization and production costs would have been considered harmful to the overall performance of the company. Today, due to the different ways companies and contracts are governed, it is not as easy to make blanket statements about the link between costs and performance. The same is true for the performance of financial markets.

Globalization is not the answer to achieving perpetual growth. It is simply the fusion of demand and supply economics.

"... globalization in combination with financial innovation (in particular of the off-balance sheet type), has significantly increased the opaqueness of the financial markets. This lack of transparency has two facets. One is the difficulty of assessing the creditworthiness of individual market participants on the basis of publicly available information. Imaginative financial structures, spreading across borders, add to the confusion."[29]

Obviously, we are facing similar, if not more severe, challenges today than in the 1920s and 30s. Today we are facing the challenge of new technologies, increasing competition and declining demand. Superficially, all these factors seem to erode employment opportunities and growth. But growth still takes place in other markets.

The main reason for the disruption is a shift in the way we produce and live. The only real problem we face is that we have again entered a different era without having an adequate concept of the measurement of economic performance.

The depression we are facing now can be overcome without the incredible sacrifices our ancestors had to face. Back then, and today, we have to cope with an evaluation problem caused by a shift in technology and in the way we work. To put it a little differently:

"The first economic revolution was not a revolution because it shifted man's major activity from hunting and gathering to settled agriculture. It was a revolution because the transition created an incentive change for mankind of fundamental proportions. The incentive change stems from the different property rights under the two systems. When common property rights over resources exist, there is little incentive for the acquisition of superior technology and learning. In contrast, exclusive property rights which reward the owners provide a direct incentive to improve efficiency and productivity, or, in more fundamental terms, to acquire more knowledge and new techniques."[30]

The cost and accounting systems we have available right now do not take into account customer behavior in the long run, and lost jobs in the short run. Profits might be influenced in both ways – by cutting jobs and decreasing demand – depending on the decisions of management.

What about the decisions of corporations and their representatives? Stiglitz argues that in debt contracts, whenever prices fell below the level expected there were transfers from debtors to creditors. These (and other) redistributive changes had large real effects, and could not be insured against because of imperfections in capital markets. Large shocks could lead to bankruptcy, and with bankruptcy (especially when it results in firm liquidation) there was a loss of organizational and informational capital. Even when the shocks were not large enough to lead to bankruptcy, they had impacts on the ability and willingness of firms to take risks.[31]

This economic view of the world finally enables us to understand the impact of a crisis on human behavior. Unfortunately, no solution is offered for the devastating effects of deflationary processes. Maybe the way we measure costs and use them as a basis for economic decision-making is one reason that we still haven't come even close to solving the problem of contractive processes.

This new way of approaching economic problems was introduced by Ronald H. Coase, who is best known for his 1937 article *The Nature of the Firm*, which introduced the concept of transaction costs to explain the nature and limits of firms.[32] But it wasn't until the 1960s and early 1970s that economists around the world began to realize the importance of his findings. Mainstream economics continued to focus on old-theory applications to fix challenging times, namely deficit spending such as investments in infrastructure.

Particularly favored were mathematical models. Some of them described downward and upward swings in the economy, with equations that were used in one-dimensional physics. Unfortunately, none of these highly complicated models are useful in the current economic crisis. Mainly, this is because we do not live in a world with perfect foresight and perfect information, as some of these models would seem to indicate.

We need a fundamentally different approach; one based on realistic micro-economic findings. To achieve this we can use an interdisciplinary approach. Reality is a matrix. Even a flower can be considered a multi-dimensional entity composed of chemical activities. So why do we still look at monetary supply as being dependent on interest rates, at GDP as being a result of consumption and production, at unemployment as a figure resulting from reported jobless claims during a specific period of time?

We agreed for too long to limit ourselves, and our actions, to policies that were effective in the distant past. We never looked back and asked why we can no longer explain commonplace phenomena.

Activities in a corporate setting can be monitored and transformed into mathematically usable figures to create a valid but complex new micro-economic foundation to the economy. Linear programming can easily provide us with an analysis of sophisticated and complicated economic settings. But since reality is a matrix, we have to find the right tools and ingredients to build our case.

In the next section of this book I will describe a simple, one-dimensional example of two contractual sales systems operating in two different scenarios – in a deflationary depression, and in better times. The tool I use in this example is quality awards being handed out to best-performing companies, and I focus on their criteria, or Key Success Factors (KSFs).

4. Apply Quality Management and Quality Awards Criteria to Economic Success

To understand the meaning and purpose of our actions, we have to rely on a specific measure of performance.[33] This is only possible if we are able to evaluate the basics of activity patterns underlying all economic transactions. The Malcolm Baldridge National Quality Award is presented annually by the president of the United States to organizations that demonstrate quality and performance excellence. Three awards may be given annually in each of six categories:

Manufacturing

Service Company

Small Business

Education

Healthcare

Non-profit

Established by Congress in 1987 for manufacturers, service businesses and small businesses, the Malcolm Baldridge Award was designed to raise awareness of quality management and to recognize US companies that have implemented successful quality management systems. The education and healthcare categories were added in 1999, and a government and non-profit category was added in 2007.

The Baldridge Award is named after the late Secretary of Commerce Malcolm Baldridge, a proponent of quality management. The US Commerce Department's National

Institute of Standards and Technology manages the award.[34]

The European Quality Award is referred to as the EFQM Excellence Award. Europe's most prestigious award for organizational excellence, it has been awarded to Europe's best-performing companies and non-profit organizations since 1992. Recipients are industry leaders with an undisputable track record of success in turning strategy into action, and in continuously improving their organization's performance.[35]

The criteria for both awards are similar, although the European award also focuses on environmental issues. In this book I blend the criteria for both awards to measure the performance of companies. The focus is on activities that have to be conducted under each criteria, or Key Success Factor, for companies to achieve higher performance.

Activities and costs are not independent of each other. To achieve higher scores, decision-makers must take specific actions at certain points in time. This analysis takes a close look at activities and their consequences for sales. I compare the character of specific activities with costs incurred in specific scenarios – after all, cost as a concept is always based on an alternative action being taken.

Some activities are riskier than others. Unfortunately, the concept of Shareholder Value as discounted cash flow does not explicitly recognize that fact. Companies were and will be sued for negligence and the negative effects of pollution, food poisoning and other unforeseen events. When things go wrong, risky activities can be very damaging to the reputation of a company, and somehow this has to be considered when looking at corporate performance. Stock markets are quick to react, and negative news tends to discount the price of stocks.

As Joseph Schumpeter said in his *Theory of Economic Development*:

"… the compensation for greater risk is only apparently a greater return: it has to be multiplied by a probability coefficient, whereby its real value is again reduced – and indeed exactly by the amount of the surplus. Anyone who simply consumes the surplus will atone for it in the course of events. Therefore, there is nothing in the independent role often attributed to the element of risk, and in the independent return sometimes connected with it."[36]

In times of mass production, concepts such as cash-flow return on investment provided a realistic contribution. Looking at our accounting practices more critically, it seems that investors are often left in doubt, or in the dark. Write-offs for outsourcing jobs do decrease costs, but do they also indicate the consequences for employees and other local resources in the long run?

Furthermore, specific activities connected to a product (pre- and after-sale) have undergone quite a transformation. The assembly line is not predominant any more – the time of mass production is over. The basic needs of consumers have already been met. We are living in a time when needs are being invented by producers.

The concept of quality has also changed. It has gone from simple quality assurance and control, to quality management. So what really defines the fiscal success of a company today?

If we want to measure business performance excellence, we have to consider quality as a benchmark. But we also have to take a closer look at the costs.

The concept of quality measurement has been improved over time, starting with the ISO standards and developing into Total Quality Management approaches.

But when evaluating a company, one way to a clearer understanding of reality is to look at activities.

Activities, the core units of economic transactions, can be classified easily. We know that functions determine activity patterns. We only have to ensure that we are looking at the actual activities being chosen and conducted. In practice, quality awards evaluate activities. Usually, companies that win these awards are among the leaders in their industry, and they generally show excellent stock market performance.

In the US, the Malcolm Baldridge Award was initiated in 1986 mainly to rescue the American market from overwhelming Japanese competition. In 1994, only 70 companies applied to be tested for excellence, although an astonishing 500,000 companies ordered the self-assessment brochure.

So why not use the criteria of quality awards to identify Key Success Factors that will help us determine Shareholder Value?

So far, all of the approaches to measuring Shareholder Value arrive at a specific number telling us where we stand. But I am convinced that we are looking at a far more complicated picture. Almost all factors are interdependent, which can be accounted for by matrix calculation and linear programming. However, for the purpose of our discussion here, I will keep it simple and reduce the problem to a one-dimensional analysis.

The most important point is to choose specific activities related to the different KSFs, such as *amount of improvement* as an indicator of sales related to the empowerment of human resources. An aggregated figure of the sales caused by specific activities will reflect the Shareholder Value of a company. Since comparisons only tell us the value of a specific number, we have to draw on other comparable industries.

The following example compares two companies that sell electronic products using two different sales systems – resale price maintenance, and franchising.

Shareholder Value (SV) is determined by the award's criteria, or by Key Success Factors that have to be added and weighted to construct an index.

$$SV = KSF : W \qquad (W = weight)$$

The ultimate solution has to be a holistic approach, so we will have to rely on concepts we already know, such as corporate culture, strategies, process management, empowerment of employees and customer satisfaction. As a result we will be able to understand that the real KSFs of a company might be disregarded, and therefore its SV will remain unknown.

In this way, using an approach based on activities as a part of KSFs, companies can reassess their performance. That way, their SV could be improved by 100 percent. This can be proven by running the figures back in time and comparing them to the actual performance of the stock markets. Furthermore, this new approach will enable us to evaluate mergers and acquisitions on a holistic basis.

Key Success Factors

If we want to have a closer look at KSFs, we must have an idea of the concepts important for the survival of companies in a competitive environment. Quality, timing and efficiency are important issues. KSFs have to be put into perspective if we want to determine Shareholder Value. Wouldn't it be much easier to have a completely new evaluation of KSFs?

We intend to look at KSFs and Shareholder Value (SV) as a problem, a number which has to be determined. But the way we interpret Shareholder Value is outdated. Most of the time this number is measured using approaches that focus on issues related to capital, but what really matters is the interaction of the company with its customers, employees, the law and the environment, along with how the company represents itself. An evaluation of a company's success comes down to an evaluation of the underlying activities that lead to an increase in sales.

Almost all accounting systems were set up 100 or more years ago. But times have changed. The age of industrialization is over. We are facing different problems in a different age – the information age. Many things have changed to meet the needs of today's businesses – we use the Internet to communicate, we send snail mail at a much faster speed, and our machines exploit our resources more efficiently than ever before.

Why hasn't the concept of Shareholder Value changed?

Any new approach will have to measure efficiency according to what a specific activity contributes to a certain goal. In other words, positive and negative contributions can be coherent with or deviate from specific goals. Coherence is an investment in the process of achieving a certain KSFs. Activities of deviation simply reduce profit. However, it is crucial to discern between those activities of deviation that do, and those that do not, affect customers.

For example, warranty costs affect customers and influence opinion about the product, but excess waste during production doesn't.

Sales Contracts

A Sales Contract is an agreement that provides for the permanent transfer of property rights (an asset) from one party to another. As mentioned earlier, this analysis will focus on contracts between producers and their retail units, such as franchising and resale price maintenance. When it comes to sales contracts, New Institutional Economics mainly focuses on pre- and post-contractual opportunism, hence analyzing the effects of cheating (non-conforming contractual behavior) by one of the parties before or after the contract is entered into. But when either of the parties do not disclose specific facts before entering into the legal agreement, they are not fulfilling the contract after being subject to its rules and obligations.

Generally, the coordination of activities depends on the content of property rights specified in a contractual setting. Sales contracts in the form of implicit contracts or complex relational contracts can be looked at as self-enforcing principal-agent relationships. Sales contracts, especially franchising, have extensive controlling rights against hidden actions from the retail sales unit.

Surprisingly enough, shareholders do not have any control over their companies if they do not hold a substantial part of the total amount of shares. This misfit between the assignment of property rights and their potential abuse by the management of a company is an example of a failure of activities being wrongfully assigned by property rights.

To determine realistic figures for an organization, its functions have to be classified. Generally, functions imply certain activities, but in reality not all activities are carried out. Therefore, we have to identify relevant operative and strategic activities in each specific contractual setting. Activities, in turn, create cost-driving processes that determine values for the company and for its customers, employees and agents. Then and only then is it possible to deduce realistic figures.

We should not forget that there is always a need for benchmarks. Benchmarks can include old activity patterns or the activities of similar processes being conducted by other companies (not necessarily competitors).

To determine KSFs we first have to look at the activities connected to each specific function, and to the specific amount of sales. Generally we can observe many activities, but to specify KSFs we have to look at the relation between sales and activities.

Usually when KSFs are determined there is little or no focus on core processes. But to properly determine KSFs, a systematic solution requires that we first isolate core processes. For example, since some administrative tasks are part of valuable core activities, whenever radical measures are taken important details about the flow of information between departments or people are at risk of getting lost. If two people working closely together in different departments have to change what they are supposed to be doing, they might still provide valuable services for the other person even though these services are not covered in the current job description. For individuals, the definition of labor is often linked to what one is supposed to do, not what one likes to do.

Functions → Activities → KSFs and Efficiency

Functions can be classified by their quantitative and qualitative natures. Companies with only qualitative functions are set up to overcome shortages and tensions created by the market. These include brokers, portfolio managers, oil company exploration departments, engineering companies and consultants. Companies with a quantitative approach are set up to create an economic balance between time, money and location. They can include distributors, transportation workers, disposition and storage workers and even banks (loans, mortgages).

The Malcolm Baldridge Quality Award

A quality award usually represents the evaluation of quality by the market, or by government rules and regulations. In the United States, the Malcolm Baldridge Quality Award introduced by the Ronald Reagan administration in 1986 was based on the criteria of leadership, strategies, process management, information and analysis, empowerment, customer satisfaction and financial results. Our focus is on the deployment of the award and its consequences for business performance excellence.

One way of looking at the determination of KSFs and SV is linear programming.

Sales Yi can be considered as a one-dimensional vector Y. This vector is determined by a matrix of activities, or KSF Xi. The more these activities are applied, the higher the sales performance, or Yi . To get a mathematical equation, we have to try to estimate the relation between Yi and Xi. Basically, we are looking at a regression model with

59

many observed activities contributing to specific KSFs. The more activities we can observe, the easier it is to draw a line approximately reflecting the relation between the two variables.

Of course, there is a deviation between the actual observed coordinates Xi/Yi and the estimated Xi/Yi. Certainly, linear programming can cope with interdependent variables. That is why we should focus on a simple descriptive approach for now, and derive activity patterns that will allow us to determine SV by creating a weighted average of the estimated sales numbers of the eight activities representing the award criteria. But first, the question we have to ask is what activities lead to a higher performance, as measured in sales?

Each company is based on specific contracts that determine the rules, rights and duties of their members. These implicit and explicit contracts are in turn governed by the functions and activities of the company. The performance of an organization can be measured by certain criteria, most likely imposed by society, by the law, by customers and by the stock markets.

In the following example, we will draw on the seven award criteria to obtain widely accepted, popular and practical measures for business performance. These measures include leadership, strategies, process management, empowerment, information and analysis, society and the law, customer satisfaction and business results.

Let's assume that two companies are selling electronic products including televisions. It has a weak culture and is pursuing a price-fixing strategy for its retailers. Company B has a strong culture. It operates on a franchise basis with its retailers, and has a marketing strategy of diversification.

Leadership

In general, the leaders of a company have to define the mission and culture (communication, design and behavior) of the company. The corporate mission of Federal Express, for example, is to deliver your package within 24 hours. This statement presents a measurable bundle of activities and sales figures. It also reflects the behavior and communicative patterns of employees and clients.

Furthermore, it proves whether the company has a weak or strong culture, which is important if leaders want to determine strategy.

A strong culture spells out how people have to behave most of the time – how they should decide to act in a given situation. In a weak culture, employees waste a good deal of time just trying to figure out what they should do and how they should do it. Strong cultures usually give guidelines and manuals to their members. As well, they provide fast decision-making processes, high motivation and loyalty, and are easily controllable. However, strong cultures can develop subcultures and other counterproductive activities that make it impossible to set up a domineering strategy.

Weak cultures, on the other hand, work well with strategic plans but often fail to represent a standardized corporate image. To achieve excellent business performance, the culture and strategy of a company have to fit. This is even more important if a merger or acquisition is being considered. A misfit can lead to a considerable decrease in sales.

If we look at companies A and B in our example, neither one really has a measurable mission. Company A has a weak culture, since price-fixing contracts are legally allowed only if a retailer is able to sell the products of other manufacturers as well. The strategy of price fixing tends to give retailer a higher margin compared to competitive products, and it suggests to the customer that the product has a higher quality than comparable products.

In this case, the compatibility between culture and strategy is no problem since we are dealing with a strong strategy dominating a weak culture.

Company B, an organization with franchised outlets, sells electronic products as well. It has a standardized corporate image with similar behavior, design and communication patterns. Customers know that wherever they go they can expect the same kind of service. Franchises require revenue-sharing by management and retailers. The compatibility between culture and strategy is fragile, but strongly supported by guidelines and manuals which give direction to each member of the organization.

To know whether we are dealing with good leadership and management of Company B, we can measure the amount of successful deliveries in one month, and the corresponding sales figures. Company A sells 90 televisions in one month, while Company B sells 150 televisions in the same period. Both figures represent the number of successful deliveries – Key Success Factors. On average, however, returned deliveries are higher in Company A. The amount of sales is $90,000 in Company A, while in Company B sales are at $140,000.

According to the Malcolm Baldridge Award, the leadership of a company accounts for 90 points out of a total of 1,000. In percentage points, that means a weighted component of the SV for Company A is 0.09 x $90,000 = $8,100, and an equivalent figure of $12,600 for Company B.

Strategies

The marketing strategy of Benetton is to confront customers with advertising pictures so shocking that the client will remember the products (think of a priest kissing a nun). The corporate culture, however, focuses on a peaceful approach: United Colors of Benetton. Because the level of tolerance toward its advertised images varies with the culture of the country in which the advertising is presented, Benetton's marketing strategy was accepted in Europe but in the United States people began complaining and even attacking its retailers. This shows that a marketing strategy has to be evaluated first, before it detracts from the corporate image.

Weak cultures do sometimes fit with a strong strategy, but quality controls and good results seem to be hard to achieve. Strong cultures and strong strategies can have bad repercussions on profits, but can be supported by underlying contracts such as in franchising. To make a strategy and a culture compatible, the strategy has to be chosen first and the culture has to support it.

Strategies are defined according to the business environment – mainly the needs of clients and their characteristics:

Location of the business

Industry of the client

Factors and reasons of purchase

Frequency of purchases

If there are no subsequent purchases even after the normal time for replacement has lapsed, and if there are high warranty costs, it is an indication that the chosen strategy must be reviewed.

The activity that confirms a chosen strategy is frequency of purchases. In other words, the strategy is measured in sales. All too often, strategic activities turn out to be costly. That is why business leaders have to guard against activities that increase costs but not company, customer or agent value. In franchising, the frequency of purchases is usually higher than in price-fixing arrangements. What makes the difference is the number of returned deliveries.

In the preceding example, the number of returns was higher for Company A than for Company B. In Company A, 10 percent of televisions were returned on average, while in Company B only eight percent were returned. As a result of its overly high returns, Company A is at risk of incurring a loss. It has to subtract the costs of repair, maintenance and storage from the number of successful deliveries.

The Malcolm Baldridge Award gives 55 points out of 1,000 to strategic planning. In this case Company A would get 0.055 x [\$8,100 - \$440] = \$7,660, while Company B would get 0.055 x [\$13,500 - \$742.50] = \$11, 857.

Process Management

In the age of industrialization, process management was restricted to facilitating mass production. Specialization was the key to success. The efficiency of the assembly line was basically the only thing that had to be taken care of. In the information age, however, generalization is the way to dominate the market. Everybody in a company should know how a product or service is produced, or at least be able to access the information.

Since the "discovery" of business re-engineering, we started to realize that processes have to be considered as simultaneous activities working together to achieve a result. The key to resolve inefficiencies – so we learned – is to reduce information deficiencies. Online and remote functions are used to produce a level of knowledge at the point of sale that is fast and efficient.

The work is done where it is efficient, not where it used to be done. Value-added merchandising concepts such as continuous replenishment and efficient consumer response are examples of re-engineering possibilities.

Wal-Mart is now in charge of managing the logistics of products manufactured and delivered by Procter & Gamble, since Wal-Mart as the distributor knows better the quantities being requested by its customers. Scanning and electronic data support these faster and more efficient processes.

Generally speaking, employees today have to know what they are selling. Microsoft is an excellent example of a company that knows how to prepare the marketplace, and its sales agents, with appropriate information before the introduction of a new product.

In general, it can be helpful to know who the lead users are, and to provide them with advance information. Flexibility can only be achieved if the latest available information is provided. The goal is to have processes that are controllable and activities that are accountable. That is why business leaders have to analyze repetitive processes and to focus on product-related processes.

There must be a differentiation between core processes and activities, and those that can eventually be outsourced. The answer to that question provides us with information about how much capacity a certain process or activity demands. Another tool to increase sales is to simulate alternative processes to determine the opportunity costs for carrying out a specific activity.

The franchise system of Company B is based on a marketing strategy of penetrating the market. It can therefore generate higher sales than the price-fixing distribution strategy for the products manufactured by Company A. The processes in Company A focus on receiving a premium for each specific product. The target is to increase the turnover of the company. The process management of Company B, however, concentrates on the standardization and competitiveness of the franchises. The target is to achieve economies of scale, since investment in the core activities of this company is high.

The pace of market penetration is a very good indicator of a successful process management. The number for Company A seems low because the percentage of customers attracted by higher prices is relatively lower than the percentage of customers attracted by the competitive corporate image of Company B.

The Malcolm Baldridge Award gives 140 out of 1,000 points to process management. Again, we can measure KSFs as market penetration in terms of sales over a specific period of time. To make the example simple, we can take the sales figures used in the first example. The component to measure SV is 0.14 x $90,000 = $12,600 for Company A, and for Company B it is 0.14 x $140,000 = $19,600.

Empowerment and Human Resources

Empowerment of employees is always considered to be an investment. Trained staff helps ensure quality control and satisfied customers. To enhance motivation along with the incentive to improve the workplace, and to develop initiatives to perform in a more efficient way, quality performance has to be visualized. In this way, an environment can be created that keeps employees more goal-oriented.

Visualization helps standardize cultural values, communication and behavior as well. Employees are able to control themselves and compete with others. The advantage for management is that it can focus on new business ventures and not need to be involved in resolving recruiting problems and settling disputes among employees.

The measurable activity (KSFs) of empowerment should be the number of improvement proposals made by employees and their effect on sales. Target costing can provide some detailed information about the data. In this way we are able to develop a relationship between empowerment performance and KSFs.

Since price fixing guarantees a relatively high premium for the sales staff, they provide some improvement ideas in Company A. But again, the contractual arrangement of Company B is superior to that of Company A because it provides more communication advantages and more flexibility.

We know that Company A sold only two televisions due to improvement proposals by sales staff during the time period considered. We also know that Company B sold 10 times more televisions thanks to specific proposals by its salespeople. This is mainly because franchise systems

67

conduct competitive programs between outlets to improve corporate turnover and staff motivation.

So what impact does this outcome have on Shareholder Value?

The Malcolm Baldridge Award gives 140 out of 1,000 points to human resources development and management. The weighted sales figure of Company A is 0.14 x $2000 = $280, while the weighted sales figure of Company B is 0.14 x $18,666.66 = $2,613.33.

Information and Analysis

No matter what resources we rely on, only one activity quantifies performance – amount of avoided waste in relation to sales. A look at the balance sheet of companies A and B tells us in both cases that the waste that must be subtracted from sales is $20,000. This "coincidence" might be explained by the fact that Company A has no strict regulations and a weak corporate culture – the contractual arrangement of price fixing is only legally allowed if products made by other manufacturers are being distributed at the same time. The relatively strong culture of Company B often leads to cheating and opportunistic activities by staff members, ultimately resulting in wasted resources.

The Malcolm Baldridge Award gives a 75-point weight, or 0.075, to waste of resources. The result for Company A is therefore $90,000 - $20,000 = $70,000 and 0.075 x $70,000 = $5,250. The result for Company B is $140,000 - $20,000 = $120,000 and 0.075 x $120,000 = $9,000.

To stay a leader in a specific industry, management has to be extremely alert.

Specific legislation, new inventions by other industries and even competitors can increase or decrease corporate sales. One activity to watch is substitute and complementary activities connected to competitive products and services. The development of digital cameras is just one example of a new invention that had a devastating impact on sales of older film camera and related appliances. On the other hand, profits in the vitamin industry and in health food stores increased dramatically when new research proved that cancer can be cured, or at least slowed, by a higher intake of these products.

There has to be a statistical indicator of the risk factors every industry is exposed to. For fast food, it is the health food industry. McDonald's was already conducting research about alternative food 20 years ago, but at that time the market was not ready. How are we going to measure these types of risks for a company?

Genichi Taguchi in 1980[37] invented a risk function that basically states that each deviation of a specific goal should be considered a progressive increase in the risk that could lead to a deterioration of the product's reliability for the customer and decreased sales for the company – in our terms, a reduced SV.

The disadvantage of this approach is that it can only measure loss that is accountable to the company itself, and not damages that occurred in the marketplace – for the customer, the environment or others.

Any Theory can also be enhanced by practice:

Amiee Chan, the CEO of Norsat International Inc., applied several risk management techniques to the struggling company, such as an employee ownership program, cost reductions and steps to increase profit at the

69

right places. She also eliminated costly top management positions and contracted mainly business partners that would provide them with higher margins. After implementing all of these changes, the company had a successful come-back in the communications market.

The advantages of looking at radical changes done by management shows us not only the impact on cost and profits but also the activities that lead to success. If it comes to risk management, accounting can provide us with documented insured activities if a company should be sued for whatever reason. We can also look at a history of events pointing to decreasing sales, in case certain potentially damaging activities occur.

Let's look again at the two companies in our example. Price fixing is legally allowed only in a specific contractual environment. Assume that the courts have already ruled against this kind of sales system, and as a result Company A suffered a major loss trying to restructure its marketing contracts. Actually, it lost 50 percent of its sales during that period of time. If we take that indicator as a benchmark, we are looking at sales of $45,000.

A weight for environmental changes and the law does not exist under the rules of the Malcolm Baldridge Award, but it does according to European Quality Awards. European Quality Awards also criticize the over-estimation of customer satisfaction by the American Awards. So let's presume a weight of 100 points, or 0.10. Company A would be looking at 0.10 x $45,000 = $4,500 in sales. Company B is more vulnerable when it comes to customer claims. We can also say that Company B is looking at a liquidated damage of 50 percent of sales, leaving the company with sales of $70,000. After the application of the weighting, 0.10 x $70,000 = $7,000 in sales.

Customer Satisfaction

The key to customer care is pre- and after-sales activities. When customers purchase a computer, they want to be sure that they are getting all the support they need after delivery and installation. The degree and amount of support and service will ultimately decide whether the client will make subsequent purchases, or recommend the product. These activities have a positive impact on sales and must be considered as KSFs.

However, we also have to consider the reaction of customers if they are not satisfied with the product or service. Polls conducted in the US service industry show that 90 percent of unhappy customers "exit," while only four percent complain.

On average, one unhappy customer tells his story to nine people. Worse, 13 percent communicate their negative experiences to more than 20 people. A decline or increase in sales can easily be linked to the degree of customer satisfaction.

Observations of customer response to an improvement in pre- and after-sales activities can provide valuable information. Applying a customer satisfaction index, we learn that because Company B represents a standardized product, customers feel more confident buying from one of the many franchise outlets. The key factor is that customers are convinced of receiving the same quality no matter where they buy. For Company B, we receive a 100 percent sales figure of $140,000. The weighting in this case should be 150 points out of 1,000, or 0.15 x $140,000, so the result for Company B is $21,000.

Company A is losing customers because occasionally quality expectations are not met. The index represents a satisfaction level of 50 percent. In terms of sales, that means 0.5 x $90,000 = $45,000 and 0.15 x $45,000 = $6,750.

Financial Results

Market penetration is one of the most important issues for a company. Market penetration allows longevity, along with the financial resources necessary to set up and sustain a brand name. Since we used the indicator of market presence before, we have to find other measures to represent financial results. Certainly financial results depend heavily on the stock market situation as well as the opinion of driving forces behind the stock market such as analysts, investors, banks, lenders, the central bank, corporate politics and politics in general.

Fundamental and technical analysis have lost most of their importance, considering the amount of liquidity flowing in and out of markets every day. Of course, ex-post almost everything can be explained by orthodox methods. But we need an instrument that can evaluate corporations ex-ante. Since transaction volume and rumors can reverse predicted prices and values, only an independent micro-economic approach can lead to valuable results.

KSFs seem to reflect the corporate capability of being flexible, of watching every movement of the market and listening to the opinion of analysts. In this case, the observable activity would be the average of effects the stock market has had on corporate sales over a certain period of time. Deviation from the corporate sales figures already determined ($90,000 and $140,000 respectively) should be the crucial numbers to look at.

Actually, Company A is doing relatively better than Company B, since franchise companies are more vulnerable to talk of corporate takeovers and mergers, and to rumors in general. In this case, the weight is 250 points out of 1,000, or 0.25. The results are $90,000 - $10,000 = $80,000 and 0.25 x $80,000 = $20,000 for Company A, and $140,000 - $100,000 = $40,000, and 0.25 x $40,000 = $10,000 for Company B.

We have now deduced eight of the most important activity patterns, or KSFs, and determined the related sales figures for both Company A and Company B. From a holistic point of view, Shareholder Value has to be a weighted average of all these factors.

Drawing upon the quality award calculations to determine the percentages (or points) for every KSF, for Company A we are looking at the following Shareholder Value:

$8,100 + $7,660 + $12,600 + $280 + $5,250 + $4,500 + $6,750 + $20,000 = $65,140.

For Company B the comparable number is:

$12,600 + $11,857.50 + $19,600 + $2613.33 + $9,000 + $7,000 + $21,000 + $10,000 = $93,670.83.

The goal is to receive a Shareholder Value as close as possible to the value of total sales during a specific period of time. Company B can therefore be considered a more secure investment than Company A.

If we apply these simple principles to any company over a specific time period and compare the results, the credibility of that company and of a financial analysis of that company can be increased.

5. Make the Economic Rescue Plan Sustainable

The world is facing another deflationary depression, with no new theories at hand offering a solution. In our earlier discussion about orthodox economic theories we re-evaluated supply-side theory, demand-side theory and deficit spending. These theories about fundamental processes in the economy are still correct, but I believe they have to be supplemented with a more holistic picture using an interdisciplinary approach. In this book I suggest one such approach using quality awards and the concept of activities to describe microeconomic behavioral patterns and their ramification on Shareholder Value and macroeconomics.

The implementation of structural change and the creation of jobs can only occur in an environment of trust. The creation of additional lending facilities such as credit unions and the transformation of businesses into co-ops can help build that trust at the grassroots level.

New industries must be planned and set up with the support of government and the people. This can create a win-win situation for entire communities and, of course, economies. Governments have to seriously consider ending subsidies for outdated industries and worse, letting those industries blackmail them into even more commitments and deeper debt. Values such as honesty, integrity, hard work and performance have to be rewarded through mechanisms such as quality awards and financial rewards at the local and federal levels.

More transparency is required to achieve all this. But at this stage, everyone knows that we cannot continue to be greedy. We are paying for our sins. For too long we focused only on one-dimensional profit maximization and economic performance. Planned or unplanned, this happened all over the world irrespective of political ideologies. This greed-driven, one-dimensional perspective led us to over-emphasize the development of mistrust along with toxic stock market instruments designed to create even more profit.

Meanwhile the general population remained in ignorance, working two or three jobs at a time, worried about the future and trying to figure out how to survive. In a world filled with anarchy, fear is unproductive. It can only persist for a certain amount of time before there is revolt or reform.

The consequences of our greed in the past decades were ignored. In some cases they were acknowledged, but almost always too late. Just ask the employees of Enron, who lost their company pensions, or the investors who believed in that stock.

That's why corporate leaders, bankers and government officials now have to shift attention to a new definition of core rules with respect to Property Rights and Stakeholder Value. If governments and central banks continue to focus only on spending and we do not start to question antiquated accounting systems and practices – the concept of Shareholder Value as a cash-flow-driven figure and a measure for corporate performance – no matter how much money we through at the problem we run the risk of only solving part of the crisis temporarily. In the long run, we have to incorporate reality in our economic theories and policies.

We need more leaders like Bill Gates, Oprah Winfrey, Warren Buffett and other philanthropists who make a practice of giving back to the community. Their success is our success, because they are investing in education and the well-being of individuals in society. For them, the bottom line is sustainability.

To achieve sustainability, a new economic theory has to emerge. This new theory will invite individuals to own shares in the company they work for, and the bank or credit union that supports their ideas. It will look at Shareholder Value as a multi-dimensional, complex variable that will not merely serve a few greedy individuals, but will guarantee financial support to future generations.

6. Enrich Shareholder and Stakeholder Value with Government Support

The problem of social cost was written about in 1960 by R.H. Coase. His account is one of the first contributions in this century to examine the environmental consequences of a company's production. Coase argued that producers have to bear the cost of polluting the environment. We all know that the monitoring of such activities is difficult – we can introduce fines and regulations but since air, sea and land are accessible to everybody, their usage is widely considered to be free.

Global warming and hard-to-enforce emission standards are another facet of this almost-unsolvable problem. It seems impossible to achieve consensus between governments that have been negotiating and bickering for decades, fighting for and against certain standards, limits and international rules.

Instead, governments should look at corporate community involvement and at social initiatives. Corporate philanthropy has realized its important role in the world. As just one example of this, UPS, the largest express carrier and package delivery company in the world, supports the delivery of humanitarian aid in former Yugoslavia.

Connecting Shareholder and Stakeholder Value is very often imbedded in corporate culture. Corporate social initiatives are assessed, and communicated internally to employees and externally to stakeholders and the general public.

Yet there is a missing link. Governments that could make this world a better place are falling far short of

79

fulfilling their duties. Companies have taken over the role of government. Governments should take their cue from good corporate citizens and apply their positive practices in legislation. There is incredible potential for cooperation in these areas through overlapping programs and improvements at the local level.

7. Create Fair Free Trade

Production costs in the developing world are considerably lower than in the developed world. Because we live in a cost-efficient world that is constantly hunting for bargains, this fact was duly noted and celebrated by stock markets. Big, multi-national corporations outsourced hundreds of millions of jobs.

The notion of free trade meant unlimited growth for countries like India and China, thanks to their labor-cost advantage. Other places, such as coffee-farming communities in South America, were also able to participate in this transfer of wealth. Free-trade agreements allowed producers to outsource production to the lowest-labor-cost markets, and to ship the products back to where they could charge premium prices and still keep consumers happy.

But what are the consequences of free trade?

To maximize their harvest, coffee farmers were paid minimum wages and exposed to toxic chemicals. Consumers learned about the unhealthy effects of sprayed coffee plants and beans, and organic coffee became a trend.

On another front, child labor was reportedly used to produce clothing and many other products in developing countries. Now, however, if a company is connected with the exploitation of children it affects their reputation.

What are the reasons behind child labor and the exploitation of people and their land? Extreme poverty!

Incredible deficits run by their governments, or simply the inability to create moderate growth and well-being without increasing net debt in the developing world, have forced parts of the general population into prostitution, crime or child labor.

H. Sautter, in analyzing the debt crisis of the developing world, concludes that it is an ethical problem of the world currency order.[38] Many developing countries were forced into stabilizing measures with expenditure reduction and switching. In Mexico, Argentina, Bolivia, Peru, Ecuador, Brazil and Venezuela, wages dropped dramatically. The daily average consumption of calories per person decreased from 0.81 percent in the 1970s to 0.08 in the 1980s. Fewer children are being sent to school, there are more restrictions on social support, no more food subsidies and fewer health benefits.

It became easier for those countries to borrow money internationally than to create their own national sources of funds. With ready access to cheap external financing, reforming taxation systems, reducing unproductive government spending, liberalizing capital markets, reforming political systems and deregulating their markets was not a priority. This negligent behavior was caused by the tempting conditions of international lending.

But can the international community be responsible for the internal polity failures of member countries? Can the International Monetary Fund prevent economically dominant countries such as the USA from having a negative impact on other countries by increasing interest rates?

Fortunately, debt management in the 1980s (the Baker Plan and the Brady Initiative) prevented the debt crisis from expanding to the industrialized world.

Now, more than 20 years later, we have a worldwide crisis!

More regulation and stricter rules alone will not solve the problem. We need a set of rules that does not allow participants and stakeholders in a contractual arrangement to produce exorbitantly negative consequences for others without bearing any consequences. Without a functioning international trading order, and with increasing protectionism, the world currency order seems to be disconnected from the real transactions that take place around the globe every day.

V. Conclusion

The crisis at hand can only be solved at the local level. The solution requires several steps, starting with the introduction of lending units such as co-ops and credit unions working in parallel with the current banking system. This is the most important step, because banks around the globe are still at risk of failure, and bank failure on that scale would cause an enormous disruption of production leading to a global standstill of production and consumption.

We have to learn from past mistakes. Almost one century ago, as a consequence of a widespread disturbance in prices, neoclassical economists suggested a decrease in wage levels to cure the Great Depression. But letting prices and wages drop did not lead to a balancing equilibrium, as politicians had hoped. On the contrary, trust in the economy vanished, and the psychological downturn made matters worse.

Deficit spending or – simply put, printing money – did help cure the symptom, but it did nothing for the disease. The disease was a structural problem, a shift from agriculture to industrialization. Today, the shift is from industrialization to technology, and money can only have a positive impact on the economy if people still trust in its core values and if property rights are well defined, allocated and executed at the same time.

Investments in infrastructure can help sustain an economy, but the economy has to be healthy to begin with, otherwise the problems will resurface after the spending spree. Usually, disruptive changes in the structure of an economy lead to changes in incentives. That change has to be reflected in property rights, contracts and the costs individuals and companies face when making decisions.

One of the main ideas in this book is to disregard the concept of costs in favor of the concept of activities that have value and are connected to entrepreneurial or individual goals. Awards already use a measurement of performance based on specific goals.

Crucial to the evaluation of businesses and therefore to economic performance is knowledge of the contractual framework of a company and its products. In this way, by the means of comparison, we can see the difference in value of contracts, companies and institutions. Property rights theory and the concept of activities are the theoretical building blocks of this analysis. Looking at the discounted cash flow of a company versus comparing the activities and contractual patterns of two companies would certainly lead to different results.

In the United States and Europe, quality awards are used to evaluate the performance of companies and to reward the best. A contractual perspective can be used to break down activity patterns into an evaluative tool to measure the Shareholder Value of a company.

Characteristics such as leadership, strategies, customer satisfaction, process management, empowerment, resources information and analysis and financial results can be used to measure performance. These characteristics and their contribution in percentage points to an overall figure can already be found in American and European quality awards programs. A weighted index of these characteristics determining how much they contribute to the sales of a company can provide a concept to measure and compare Shareholder Value.

This book does not claim to offer a complete answer. The measurement of Shareholder Value requires predetermined weights and percentage points. Nevertheless, we have a foundation in existing quality awards, and an overall application would certainly help to shed some light on the difficulty to measure performance.

Certainly, more research has to be done. There is an enormous lack of compatibility between applied accounting and reality. The change that has to occur has to tackle deep, underlying problems. An overhaul of our accounting systems has to address uncomfortable issues – accounting practices used for window dressing in big corporations that present themselves in the way that they want to be seen, for example. A good example of this is Enron.

We should not let old, antiquated cost accounting and Shareholder Value systems ruin the lives of millions of people. When insider knowledge and flows determine the rise and fall of values and markets, something is terribly wrong with the measurement of corporate performance and its impact on us. Still, advisors continue to sell products and investments and it seems they did not know any better. Unfortunately, we have now reached a point in the evolution of the current financial crisis where the crash of equity and home markets is turning into a form of expropriation – a terrible situation that will leave entire generations penniless and jobless. That's why the concept of Shareholder Value has to be examined and improved. Shareholder Value has to embrace the measurement of quality, empowerment, environmental responsibility and more.

We also have to look again at the past: mismanagement and overspending by public authorities can lead to inflationary pressures that worsen the crisis. Credibility is key. Credibility regarding our international trading partners and their policies is also important – strings have to be attached to cheap money from international lenders. These strings must ensure that some eccentric leaders can't simply pocket the funds while their populations are starving.

Major disruptions throughout history, such as the Great Depression in the 1920s and 1930s and the tulip hysteria with inflated tulip prices in the Netherlands centuries ago, provide lessons if we study the mistakes. We have to learn from those mistakes. We must acknowledge the mistakes that led to the present financial disaster. Greed can be controlled, but there must be general consensus about values and business practices.

A discussion about the validity of interest rates, the abuse of financial power and the need for regulation has been going on for thousands of years. Money was not imposed on us and money itself is not creating our problems. Unfortunately, technology in the form of the Internet has increased the monetization of nearly everything, and at the same time it has increasingly depersonalized our interactions. Yet I believe a change in our collective conscience is happening right now. It is telling everyone, all over the world, that we cannot continue like this. Every crisis can be looked at as a problem, or as a challenge for change. Let us look at this crisis as a historic learning experience, one that will lead the way to a better future.

Although this book cannot provide all the answers to all the questions being raised today, it can try to launch a much-needed discussion about the need for alternative methods to measure economic performance. It can call, loud and clear, for a new economic theory.

VI. Literature

Beck, P., The Truth about Shareholder Value – A Solution to Deflationary Depression, Medu Verlag, Schloss Phillipseich, Germany, 2004

Beck, P., Unbequeme Wahrheiten ueber den Sharholder Value, Orell-Fuessli, Zuerich, Switzerland 2006

Brunner, E., Lorge, I., Rural Trends in Depression Years: A Survey of Village-Centered Agricultural Communities, 1930-1936, New York, Columbia University Press,1937

Burtchett, F.F., Floyd F., "Unorganized Speculation: The Possibility of Control," American Economic Review, vol.27, 1937

Christensen, C., Craig, T., Hart, S., "The Great Disruption," in: Foreign Affairs,

March/ April 2001, Vol. 80, Number 2

Coase, R.H., "The Nature of the Firm," *Economica*, 4 (1937): 386-405

Coase, R.H., "The Problem of Social Cost," Journal of Law and Economics, 3, 1960, 1-44

T. Deal, A. Kennedy, Corporate Cultures, (Reading, Massachusetts, 1982)

Demsetz, H., "Information and Efficiency: Another Viewpoint,": Journal of Law & Economics, 12, 1969, 1-22

Eckes, A., "Is Globalization Sustainable?" US News and World Report, Feb.11 2002

Fisher, F.M., McGowan, J.J., "On the Misuse of Accounting Rates of Return to Infer Monopoly Profits" in American Economic Review, vol. 73, 1983

Furubotn, E. G., Richter, R., Institutions and Economic Theory. The Contribution of the New Institutional Economics, Ann Arbor, The University of Michigan Press, 1997

Hammer, M., Beyond Reengineering, New York, Harper Collins, 1996

Hammer, M., Champy, J., Business Reengineering, New York Harper Collins, 1994

Hesse, H., Issing, O., Geld und Moral (Money and Ethics), Verlag Vahlen, 1994, Munich

Hicks, J.R., "Mr. Keynes and the Classics," Econometrica, 5, 1937, Chicago

Hoffman, W.G., "Control of Speculation under the Securities Exchange Act," The American Economic Review, 1937

Hooper, F.W., The Functions of a Bank in Relation to the Capital Market: A Discussion of Some Criticism of the London Capital Market in its Relation with British Industry, and of a Suggested Line of Remedial Action by the Joint Stock Banks, London: Gee, 1936

Keynes, J.M., The General Theory of Employment, Interest and Money, Macmillan Cambridge Univeristy Press for the Royal Economic Society, The Collected Writings of John Maynard Keynes, First Edition 1936, 1973

Kirshman, J.E., Review of Laufenburger, H., Methoden der krisenabwehr und der Konjunkturpolitik in Frankreich, Jena: Fischer, 1936, in American Economic Review, vol.27, 1937

Mayer, M., The Fed. The Inside Story of How the World's Most Powerful Financial Institution Drives the Markets, Penguin Putnam Inc., New York, 2002

Nogaro, B., La Crise Economique dans le Monde et en France: Symptomes, Causes et Remedes, Lib. Gen. de Droit et de Jurisprudence, 1936

North,D.C., Institutions, Institutional Change, and Economic Performance. Cambridge University Press, 1990

North, D.C., Thomas, R.P., The First Economic Revolution, Economic History Review, vol. 30, 1977

O'Byrne, S.F., Operating Performance and Shareholder Value, www.valueadvisors.com/operating_performance.htm

Oi, W.Y., Productivity in Distributive Trades: The Shopper and the Economies of Massed Reserves, Economic and Legal Organization Workshop, University of Rochester, 1990

Reid, A., Shakedown. How the New Economy is Changing Our Lives, Seal Books, McClelland-Bantam, Inc., Toronto, 1996

Schumpeter, Joseph A., The Theory of Economic Development, translated Redvers Opie (Cambridge, MA: Harvard University Press, 1936, pp. 85, 86)

Smith, A., An Inquiry into the Natures and Causes of The Wealth of Nations, (1776), edited, with an introduction, notes, marginal summary, and enlarged index by Edwin Cannan (Random House, Modern Library Edition, 1994)

Stiglitz, J.E., Information and the Change in the Paradigm in Economics, in: American Economic Review, vol.92, 2002

Taguchi, G., Introduction to Quality Engineering. Designing Quality into Products and Processes, Dearborn: American Suppliers Inc., 1986

Wallis, J.J., North, D.C., Measuring the Transaction Sector in the American Economy, 1870-1970, in: Engerman and R.E. Gallman, Long-Term Factors in American Economic Growth, 95-161. Studies in Income and Wealth, no.51, Chicago and London: University of Chicago Press, 1988

Williamson, O.E.,The Economic Institutions of Capitalism (New York, Free Press, 1985)

www.nationalawards.com

www.efqm.org

Footnotes

1 www.TheGreatWesternBreweryCompany:Adjustment.ca

2 www.vancouverisland.com

3 Smith, A. (1776), reprinted 1994; An Inquiry into the Natures and Causes of The Wealth of Nations

4 Smith, A., p. 4

5 Smith, A., p.33

6 Smith, A., p.34

7 "The word value, it is to be observed, has two different meanings, and sometimes expresses the utility of some particular object, and sometimes the power of purchasing other goods which the possession of that object conveys. The one might be called "value in use"; the other, "value in exchange". Smith, A., p.31

8 Smith, A., p.35

9 Stiglitz, J.E. (2002),"Information and the Change in the Paradigm in Economics", in American Economic Review, vol.92 no.3, p.478

10 Stiglitz, J.E. (2002),"Information and the Change in the Paradigm in Economics", in American Economic Review, vol.92 no.3, p.460, p.462

11 Kirshman, J.E., Review of Laufenburger, H., Methoden der Krisenabwehr und der Konjunkturpolitik in Frankreich, Fischer, Jena, 1936 in: American Economic Review, 1937, vol. 27, p.132

12 Keynes, J.M., The General Theory of Employment, Interest and Money, Macmillan Cambridge University Press For the Royal Economic Society, The Collected Writings of John Maynard Keynes, First Edition 1936, 1973

13 Keynes, J.M., p.260-261

14 Keynes, J.M. p. 262

15 Keynes, J.M., p.263

16 Burtchett, Floyd F.,"Unorganized Speculation: The Possibility of Control", American Economic Review, 1937, vol. 27, p.288 and 289

17 Hoffman, W.G.,"Control of Speculation under the Securities Exchange Act", The American Economic Review, 1937, vol. 27, p.279

18 Nogaro, Bertrand, La Crise Economique dans le Monde et en France: Symtomes, Causes et Remedes. Lib. Gen. De Droit et de Jurisprudence. 1936

19 Hicks, J.R., Mr. Keynes and the 'Cassics'", Econometrica, April 1937, vol.5

20 Mayer, M., The Fed. The Inside Story of How the World's Most Powerful Financial Institution Drives the Markets, Penguin Putnam Inc., New York, 2002

21 Furubotn, E.G., Richter, R. (1997)

22 Hooper, F.W., The Functions of a Bank in Relation to the Capital Market: A Discussion of Some Criticism of the London Capital Market in its Relation with British Industry, and of a Suggested Line of Remedial Action by the Joint Stock Banks, London, Gee. 1936

23 Jeremiah, D.B., The Causes and Prevention of the Corporate Bond Default. A Thesis. Philadelphia, University of Philadelphia, 1936

24 Brunner, E., Lorge, I., Rural Trends in Depression Years: A Survey of Village-Centered Agricultural Communities, 1930-1936, New York, Columbia University Press, 1937

25 Wallis, J.J. and North, D.C., Measuring the Transaction Sector in the American Economy, 1870-1970. In S.L. Engerman and R.E. Gallman, eds., Long-Term Factors in American Economic Growth, 95-161. Studies in Income and Wealth, no.51 Chicago and London: University of Chicago Press.1988, p.122

26 Oi, W.Y."Productivity in the Distributive Trades:The Shopper and the Economies of the Massed Reserves." Economic and Legal Organization Workshop, University of Rochester. Mimeo, 1990, p.4

27 O'Byrne, S. F., Operating Performance and Shareholder Value, www.value advisors.com/operating_performance.htm, 1998

28 Reid, A., Shakedown. How the New Economy is Changing our Lives, Seal Books, McClelland-Bantam, Inc., Toronto, 1996

29 In Forrest Capie, Charles Goodhart, Stanley Fischer, and Norbert Schadt, The Future of Central Banking. Tercentary Symposium of the Bank of England (Cambridge: University Press, 1995), p.336

30 North, D.C., Thomas, R.P., 1977, "The First Economic Revolution," Economic History Review, 30, 229-241, p.240-241

31 Stiglitz,2002, p.482

32 Coase, R.H., 1921,"The Nature of the Firm", in: Economica, 4, 386-405

33 Beck, P., 2004

34 http://www.quality.nist.gov/

35 http://www.efqm.org

36 Schumpeter, Joseph A., The Theory of Economic
    Development, trans Redvers Opie (Cambridge, MA:
    Harvard University Press, 1936, pp. 85,86)

37 Taguchi Genichi, 1980, p 23

38 Sautter, H. in Hesse, Issing, Money and Ethics, 1994, p.104